Genre Realistic Fiction

I0800076

Essential Question

How do new experiences offer new perspectives?

Silver Linings

by Susan Paris
illustrated by Soud

Chapter 1 Clouds

“Every cloud has a silver lining.” It drives me crazy when Mom says nonsense like that. I’d barely had time to hobble to the car and arrange myself in the passenger seat, my throbbing foot already blown up like a balloon when she comes out with it, exactly as I knew she would. First, she pats my leg, and then she just can’t help herself: “Every cloud has a silver lining, you know, honey.”

“Mom,” I grumble, “I appreciate the thought, but I’m not ready to look on the bright side of this debacle.”

She apologizes, and I can tell she means it, but it’s pretty obvious her timing is way off; we haven’t even left the school parking lot yet.

On the farthest side of the field, I can see my teammates doing sprints as they train. As I continue watching, Coach Zito strides back toward them. He’d mercifully helped me to the car in silence. Unlike Mom, he knew when it was best to say nothing—he knew what was at stake.

As Mom starts the engine, I imagine my teammates cooling down without me while they listen to one of Coach Zito's pep talks. And next Thursday, they'll go to practice without me; and the Thursday after that …

When I had fallen and twisted my ankle, I'd cried from the pain, but now I'm crying out of self-pity. Hours and hours of training, and now this. I tell myself there's a glimmer of hope that everything will turn out okay, that I'll make it to the track-and-field meet next month, but I know it's just that: a glimmer.

The tears fall hot and fast; I drag the back of my hand under my nose and sniff loudly. Mom gives me a weak smile. "It'll be okay, Casey. You'll see."

I suspect this is another version of the silver-lining thing, but I feel so miserable that I let it pass. I mean, what's the point?

Mom has already called the medical center, so we don't have to wait to be seen. Doctor Van Dyk asks me some questions and then gently picks up my foot and moves my ankle around a bit before carefully lowering it.

I get straight down to business and nervously ask how long it will be before I can run.

"Four weeks maybe, possibly five," he answers, "and even then, you'll need to take it easy for a while. Is that possible?" he asks with a smile. He knows me well.

I can't answer. My eyes fill with tears, my throat begins to tighten, and I have to focus on his brightly patterned shirt so that I don't start crying again.

I'm exhausted, and it's a relief to get home. Chris must have heard the keys in the front door because he comes flying down the stairs two at a time, a habit that always irritates Mom. She's warned him hundreds of times not to do that because he could … sprain an ankle!

Chris takes one look at my face, and then after glancing at Mom, he follows her pointed gaze down to my foot.

"Your ankle looks like it swallowed a tennis ball!"

"Yeah, something like that," I mutter.

"Does it hurt?"

"No. Actually, it tickles," I say. In truth, I crossed my pain threshold hours ago, but I'm not about to admit it.

"No need to be sarcastic," Chris says, pretending his feelings have been hurt. "I was only asking." He gives me a sympathetic smile and heads off to raid the refrigerator.

I swing through to the den, thumping along like some kind of oversized, uncoordinated bug. Doctor Van Dyk said I would probably only need crutches for a week or so, but already my hands hurt and my shoulders ache.

I collapse onto the sofa, toss the crutches aside, and reach for the television remote.

STOP AND CHECK

How do the different characters in this chapter react to Casey's situation?

Chapter 2
"No Way!"

Kim calls me as soon as she hears. "You poor thing," she commiserates, "you must feel *totally* ripped off!"

Despite everything, I smile. Kim is allergic to exercise—she couldn't run a mile to save herself—but somehow she understands how much track means to me.

We spend the next ten minutes discussing my rotten luck, then Kim says something completely unexpected.

"Maybe this is a chance to try something new," she suggests. "You know, silver linings and all that."

My eyes instantly narrow with suspicion: "Have you been talking to my mom?"

"No … What are you talking about?"

From her tone, I can tell she's innocent. "It doesn't matter. What were you going to say?"

"Well, we need help with the school play."

"The play? No way! That's so not my scene. Plus, I'm on crutches, remember? Not to mention, I'm a terrible actor!"

"I wasn't thinking of acting. We need a prompter, and they just sit around—perfect!" Kim replies.

"Sitting around doesn't really sound like me, either."

"True," Kim says with a laugh, "but please please give it a try. We're desperate, and I could really use my best friend's help."

It's emotional blackmail, and Kim knows it. I don't know why I'm so reluctant; maybe it's because I'm not ready to accept that I won't be competing at the track meet. But it's more than that: I'm just not what teachers call a "team player." While other kids seem to love doing stuff together, that's just not me.

"Casey?" Kim's voice reminds me that while I'm not much of a people person, I still need her in my life.

I heave a dramatic sigh and ask, "So, what does a prompter do, anyway?"

Less than 24 hours later, Kim is guiding me down the stairway of the darkened auditorium.

I look around at all the kids talking and laughing and tell Kim I'm feeling kind of phobic.

"Phobic?" Kim asks. "What is there to be scared of?"

I point at all the people and explain that I'm used to being in the open air. Why is there such a crowd?

"It's a play, silly, it doesn't happen on its own." And she drags me over to introduce me to Mr. Leshko, the director.

Mr. Leshko seems grateful for my help. He gives me a script, explains what to do, and then leaves me to it. So does Kim, who disappears off to the dressing rooms.

It turns out that being the prompter isn't as heinous as I'd thought it might be. Basically, all I have to do is listen carefully and remind people of their lines when they forget them. I pick up the role pretty quickly. And I soon see why they need me. The actors mess up all the time, and I'm yelling out so many lines, I have to ask for a glass of water. The actors must be used to it though because they don't seem to mind.

Kim comes by later to ask how it went.

"Pretty well," I admit, "but I think they need more training. They forgot tons of lines!"

"Actors don't train, they rehearse," she corrects.

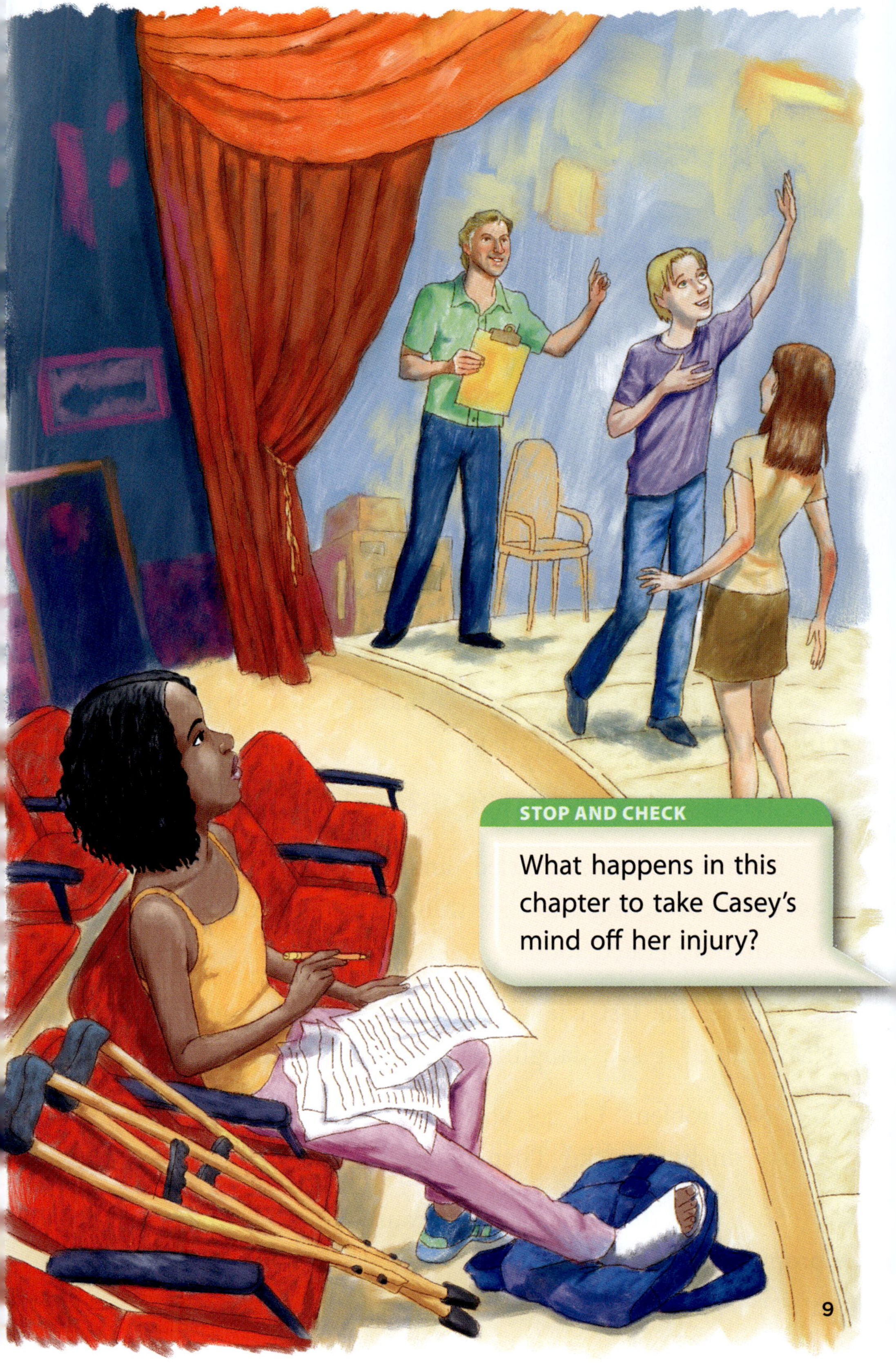

STOP AND CHECK

What happens in this chapter to take Casey's mind off her injury?

Chapter 3
Break a Leg

The following week, everybody seems to be coming down with the flu, which is how I get conned again.

"Casey," Mr. Leshko says, "Amanda's sick, so could you fill in for her at rehearsal today?"

"But she plays the sheriff," I squeak, "and I can't act."

He asks if I've ever tried, and I have to admit I haven't—but acting isn't my thing. Mr. Leshko just gives me an exasperated look.

I have one last chance of escape, and it's a good one: "My ankle," I say, dangling it limply between us.

"No problem. I'll get you a chair, and you can pretend you're on horseback." Then he's gone, just like that.

So I play the sheriff, and because I've been the prompter, I know the lines. I even do a pretty good job.

Mr. Leshko notices. After rehearsal, he walks over. "Good work, Casey. Did you enjoy yourself?"

And I have to confess, it was okay.

Dad picks me up and drives me home past the running track. Feelings of frustration and disappointment overwhelm me. The team will begin training for the 1500 meters soon—my best event. Last year, I came in second, while this year, I'll come in nowhere.

Dad senses my gloomy thoughts, and lowering the volume on the radio, he asks when the play opens.

"In three weeks, but lots of the actors are still messing up their lines, so it could be a disaster."

"I don't know; a lot can happen in three weeks. And why are you being so negative, anyway?"

"Because I'm not into acting. What's the point?"

Dad is on to me immediately. "You mean what's the point when there are no winners or losers?"

"Well, at least when I train, I get results. The kids who are trying to act are still making mistakes."

"Maybe they're simply having fun," Dad suggests. "Life is not all about winning prizes, you know."

"Huh!" I mutter—as if having fun is any consolation for missing out on competing in the track-and-field meet.

Amanda misses the next rehearsal and then the one after that too. I progress from crutches to an ankle brace and can move around the stage, and Mr. Leshko starts giving me directions. Kim thinks it's hysterical.

"You know," Kim comments after my fifth time filling in for Amanda, "you're actually really good." And she warns me to watch out. "Amanda's not indispensable," she cautions. "You're just as talented as she is."

Has Mr. Leshko been waiting in the wings for just this moment? Suddenly he's there, like he's personally scripted the scene himself.

"Kim's right," he says. "I need you to take the role permanently. Amanda won't be back in time."

"I can't," I remind him. "My limp …"

"I'll write it into the play," Mr. Leshko replies and asks Kim to help me practice my lines.

The sheriff is assisted by a deputy, who is played by Ethan Sosnowski. Everybody adores Ethan. But when he suggests we run through our scenes together, I'm surprised and automatically refuse.

"What is it with you?" Ethan asks, exasperated. "Oh, I forgot, you're a big track-and-field hotshot. I guess it's no fun if you're not the star of the show, huh?"

Ethan sees my face and hastily apologizes: "Sorry, Casey; I didn't mean it."

"That's okay," I mumble. "Most people would have the same perception of me."

He relaxes into a grin. "Probably. So do you want to practice or not, hotshot?"

Only someone totally clueless would turn him down twice, and he is kind of cute …

"Be careful, you almost looked as if you were having fun out there today," Kim teases me on the way home.

"We were only practicing our blocking," I insist weakly.

"Whatever you say!" Kim dismisses my excuse with a smile. "Only three days to go. Can you believe it?"

What I can't believe is the tingle of excitement I feel when I think about opening night.

Before our first performance, Ethan tells me to break a leg. I glare at him. Is he trying to be funny?

"It's what actors say—it's figurative," he explains. "It means good luck."

"Really?" And I start snorting with laughter. "Imagine saying 'Break a leg' to someone before the 1500 meters."

Ethan starts laughing, too, until we're both laughing so hysterically that the stage manager shoots us a dirty look.

I hate waiting, and I confess that I'm feeling nervous.

"You don't look nervous to me," Ethan observes, and then he gently pushes me onto the stage and into the glaring brightness of the spotlights.

I'm not sure who is the most enthusiastic about opening night: Mr. Leshko or my family.

"You all looked so *relaxed*." Mr. Leshko nods approvingly, and I can tell he's impressed.

"When did you learn to lasso like that?" Dad asks.

"Stop it, everybody," interrupts Chris, "or she'll get a swollen head to match her swollen ankle."

"Chris!" says Mom. "Well, I think it's great that Casey is learning she has more talents than just running."

"And the best part is that we get to do it again tomorrow night," Ethan adds. "And every night this week!"

"True." I smile. I hadn't thought of that.

"Hey, look, she's smiling!" Chris says. "Does anyone have a camera to record this momentous event?"

Dad does, of course, and we line up: Kim on one side of me, Ethan on the other. Maybe being part of a group isn't as scary as I'd thought.

STOP AND CHECK

How do the events in this chapter show how Casey has changed since the beginning of the story?

Respond to Reading

Summarize

Summarize how a new experience changes Casey's perspective in *Silver Linings*. Your graphic organizer may help.

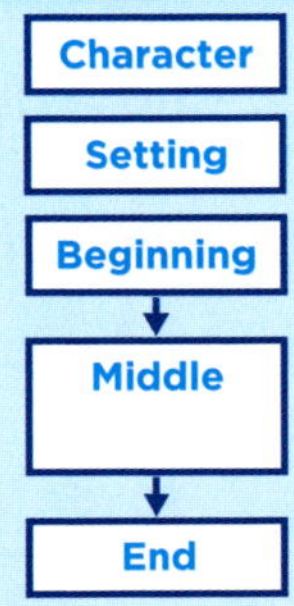

Text Evidence

1. What features of *Silver Linings* tell you it's realistic fiction? **GENRE**

2. How does Casey feel about drama when Kim first asks her to help out? How does she feel about it by the end of the story? **COMPARE AND CONTRAST**

3. What does *commiserates* on page 6 mean? Use clues in the sentence to figure it out. **SENTENCE CLUES**

4. Write, from Kim's point of view, about the changes she sees happening in her friend Casey throughout the story. **WRITE ABOUT READING**

Genre | **Personal Narrative**

Compare Texts

Read about a group of students whose perspectives change when they get lost on a hike.

THE BIG TREK

When I was 17, I spent a summer at an outdoor education center miles from anywhere, deep in the forest. We spent the whole vacation hiking, kayaking, and orienteering. The emphasis was on challenging ourselves and teamwork, and I loved every minute of it.

In our second week, our instructor, Daniel, took us on a three-hour hike. Halfway through, we stopped for a snack by a waterfall. Daniel gave us directions for getting back and told us to remember all the skills we'd been taught. He explained that he would be leaving us, but we weren't really listening: we were too busy having fun.

It was not until Daniel had left that we realized we had no idea how to get back. Some people wanted to go right; others wanted to go left; one guy was adamant that Daniel had said to follow the stream. The minutes ticked by, and one girl began crying.

Then one of the boys suggested we divide into two groups. The arguing intensified, especially when it seemed that several people really wanted to go with this suggestion. I was scared: if we went in different directions, then who knew where we would end up?

Then someone made the point that we knew where the stream ended up: it cut under a footbridge beside the center. So if we stuck together, and followed the stream, we'd get back; right?

Following the stream was difficult and painstakingly slow, but we had to pull together: we couldn't afford to give in to our fears. The slowest person was put near the front, the more confident ones led the way, and everybody shared snacks and encouraged each other.

Finally, two hours overdue, we arrived at the center just as search parties were gathering. We felt deeply embarrassed, but although we had chosen the wrong route, we were praised for sticking together.

That hike was many summers ago. Although it was a scary time, I don't regret the experience. It taught me that small acts of kindness can go a long way—I still remember how good that trail mix tasted out there in the wilderness because we had shared it.

Make Connections

What does the experience of being lost in the woods teach the hikers in *The Big Trek* about working as a team? **ESSENTIAL QUESTION**

How does looking at a problem from a different perspective change the outcomes for Casey in *Silver Linings* and for the group of hikers in *The Big Trek*? **TEXT TO TEXT**

Focus on Literary Elements

Dialogue Dialogue is used in fiction to show exactly what the characters say. It is also used to move the plot along. Dialogue *shows* what a person is saying and doing, so the author does not have to *tell* or explain everything.

The verbs the author uses instead of *said* can give clues about a character's feelings and personality.

Read and Find On page 7, Casey's reaction to Kim's suggestion that she help with the play shows what she thinks of the idea: "The play? No way! That's so not my scene." The dialogue between Casey and Kim shows that Kim really needs help, but that Casey is very reluctant.

In the dialogue between Ethan and Casey on pages 13 and 14, readers learn a lot about the changes that are taking place for Casey, as well as her reaction to Ethan's gentle teasing.

Your Turn

Write some dialogue to show what happens when Casey's ankle has healed and she goes back to the track team. How will you show her feelings through dialogue? Can you use dialogue to show how her coach and teammates react to having her on the team again?

In your own writing, remember to look for places where dialogue could show your readers what happens and what characters are like.